POP
PARTY

POP
PARTY

40 fabulous cake pops, props, and cakes

Clare O'Connell

CICO BOOKS
LONDON NEW YORK

Published in 2012 by CICO Books

An imprint of Ryland Peters & Small
519 Broadway, 5th Floor, New York NY 10012
20–21 Jockey's Fields, London WC1R 4BW
www.cicobooks.com

10 9 8 7 6 5 4 3 2 1

A CIP catalog record for this book is available from
the Library of Congress and the British Library.

ISBN: 978-1-908170-26-2

Printed in China

Editor: Miriam Catley
Photographer: Nichole Rees
Props: Kamila Maslowska
Illustration: Clare O'Connell

For other picture credits, please see page 128.

NOTE

All spoon measurements are level unless
otherwise specified.

Both imperial and metric measurements have
been given. Use one set of measurements only
and not a mixture of both.

All eggs are US large (UK medium) unless
otherwise stated. This book contains recipes
made with raw eggs. It is prudent for more
vulnerable people, such as pregnant and
nursing mothers, babies and young children,
invalids and the elderly, to avoid uncooked
dishes made with eggs.

Some of the recipes contain nuts and should not
be consumed by anyone with a nut allergy.

Ovens should be preheated to the specified
temperatures. All ovens work slightly differently.
We recommend using an oven thermometer and
suggest you consult the maker's handbook for
any special instructions, particularly if you are
cooking in a fan-assisted oven, as you will
need to adjust temperatures according to
manufacturer's instructions.

Contents

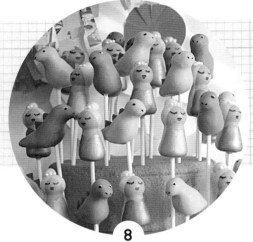

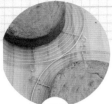

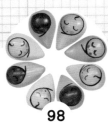

introduction

2010 was an amazing year for the O'Connells—our house was turned upside down by me and my POPs. 2011 has seen POP Bakery only continue to grow!

The POP Bakery has now moved from a tiny room in the back of our suburban house to a large room in the front. When I think about that small room now, I really don't know how we managed to turn over 300 POPs a day in such a tiny space!

However, it was a very exciting time, and I didn't dare turn down an order, so working 14 hours a day became the norm. The only good thing about that room was the beautiful "jungle" garden it looked on to, which my dad has been landscaping for the last year and a half. I like to think of the new room as my studio—random paper flowers, tassels, and piñatas hang from the window, just like the ones you'll see in this book.

Our team, as well as our space, expanded in 2011. Whereas in the previous year I worked with an old friend and my parents, since then we have welcomed all sorts of talented people into the POP team. We have a great setup now— working just nine hours a day, eating homemade lunches, and chatting endlessly as we roll, dip, and paint POPs all day.

It's been a real learning curve for a 23-year-old girl, but the business has gone from strength to strength. We have a lovely client base, people who use us all the time, and we're still gaining new customers every day, through word of mouth

Dad's "jungle" garden.

and from all the wonderful publications that have so kindly featured us since we began this exciting venture.

Our designs for POPs have improved vastly—hope you agree! I have found new ways of painting the POPs, which are far better than before, and all the new developments are included in this book.

As well as delicious and beautiful POPs and cakes, *POP Party* also includes some fabulous PROPs—projects that go with your POPs and cakes to create the perfect sweet table. Having been inspired by both the event companies and the creative art students whom we've worked with this year, I discovered a passion for party decorations, which I've shared with you here. It's been such fun to research different party themes and style shoots for the book. None of the PROPs are too tricky—you just need the right equipment, which is readily available from many stores and websites, all of which can be found on our extensive suppliers list.

I am over the moon about the first book being such a success—so many of you have emailed me to say how much you have enjoyed using it, and these are always my favorite emails to receive. I do hope you love this book, too—blood, sweat, and tears have gone into it, for sure!

I hope you enjoy this book, and I wish you happy POPing and PROPing!

Find out how to make Apple POPs on page 60.

These Popsicle POPs can be found on page 30.

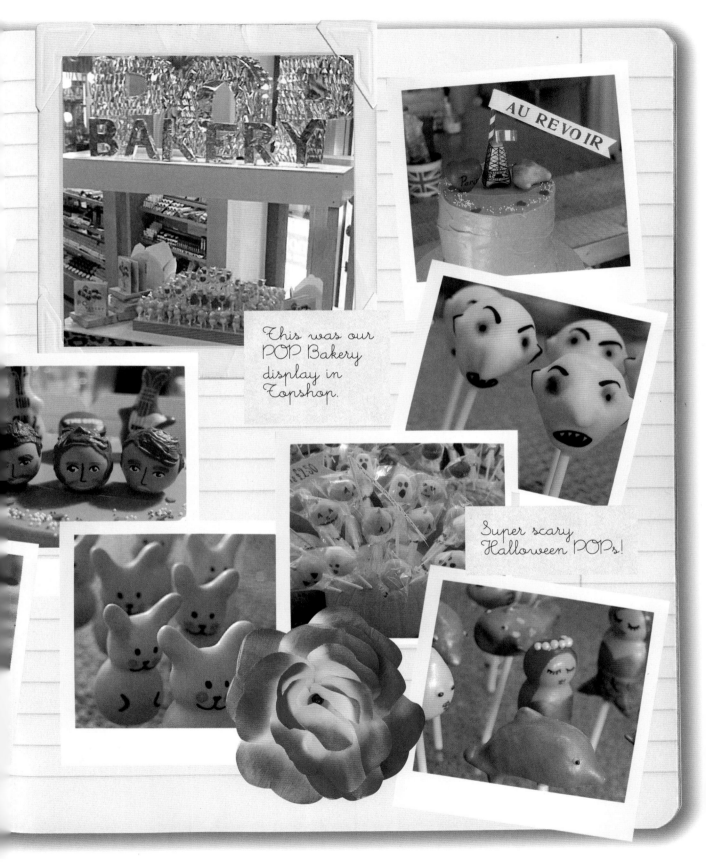

This was our POP Bakery display in Topshop.

Super scary Halloween POPs!

Be creative with your POPs—just about any design is possible!

Make your own Cake Slice POPs on page 34.

POP Parties

When it comes to the main event, there are so many ways in which you can display your POPs. As you'll see, at the POP Bakery I have a metal frame for them, but you can use a polystyrene block, too. They also look great standing in a simple glass or preserve jar, as below—or why not have a go at making a cake stand (see page 38)?

Usually when I make POPs, I make them all in one design, but sometimes a party display looks even better with a variety of POPs together—here, I've mixed Mermaid POPs (see page 52) and Baby POPs (see page 98).

POP
Secrets

POP shop

There are a few items that you need to have for your POP-making experience. Most are standard pieces of kitchen equipment, but you may need to visit a specialty cake store or search online for some of the more unusual ingredients.

POP EQUIPMENT

• *Food processor*—this helps to speed up the cake-making process, and is useful for mixing the cream cheese frosting. You can, however, do both of these by hand.

• *Microwave*—for melting the candy melts.

• *Digital measuring scales*—to ensure that each POP is the same weight and size.

• *Lollipop sticks*—the essential piece of equipment to transform a cake ball into a POP! See page 125 for suppliers.

• *Paintbrush*—ideally in a selection of sizes, including several with fine tips for adding delicate details and thicker ones for brushing on edible dusting powder.

• *Palette*—a plate, porcelain egg cup, or clean paint palette for mixing colored dusting powders (see page 26). Please note, the paints may stain. Alternatively, use plastic wrap (clingfilm).

• *Polystyrene block or colander*—for standing your POPs in until they set. You can often find polystyrene

blocks in protective packaging. Make a few holes in readiness for your dipped POP.

• *Lollipop covers*—made from cellophane wrap and available online (see page 125 for suppliers.) Covered POPs also look great gift-wrapped with a twist of ribbon.

• *Silicon molds*—available from cake stores in a huge variety of shapes, such as flowers, butterflies, and lips.

• *Cookie (pastry) cutters*—for cutting perfect shapes.

POP INGREDIENTS

•**Candy melts**—wafers of colored candy that you melt in the microwave to form a liquid paste for dipping. They are available in 14 oz (400 g) packages in a variety of colors and are very simple to use. Melt following the package instructions, dip in your POP, and when the coating has set, it makes the perfect base for decoration. Candy melts have a vanilla flavor, or choose the cocoa version for a chocolate flavor. Thin with vegetable oil: you will need a substantial amount to thin a whole packet of candy melts. I usually pour in about 2 tablespoons at a time and keep mixing in until it becomes as smooth as melted chocolate, and creates a ribbon when you pour from a spoon.These keep well, so if you melt too many, just cover in plastic wrap (clingfilm) and keep at room temperature until your next POPing session.

•**Dipping solution/ rejuvenator spirit**—mix this with confectioner's glaze and edible dusting powder to paint details on POPs. Clear alcohol or clear vanilla extract can also be substituted for dipping solution.

•**Confectioner's glaze**—mix with dipping solution/ rejuvenator spirit and edible dusting powder to paint details on POPs.

•**Leaf glaze**—an alternative to dipping solution/ rejuvenator spirit for mixing with edible dusting powder.

•**Sprinkles (hundreds and thousands)**—there is a huge variety of sprinkles to choose from to transform a plain POP into something POPtastic!

•**Food coloring**—best to buy gel ones because these are better colors for your frosting (icing) on the POP cakes!

•**Edible dusting powders**— also known as edible tints, these are the most versatile colored powders for decorating your POPs and are best applied with a paintbrush. Apply dry onto sugar flowers or mixed with the dipping solution/glaze mixture straight on to POPs.

•**Fondant (royal icing)**—this thick, ready-made frosting can be molded into any shape you choose, from little balls for eyes to more detailed shapes using silicon molds. Mix with a little gum tragacanth (see below) to ensure that your piece hardens and keeps its shape.

•**Gum tragacanth**—a cake decorating ingredient made from natural gum that is mixed with fondant (royal icing) to make a stronger base that holds its shape well—ideal for modeling.

Candy melts and edible
dusting powders come in
a variety of colors.

Use sprinkles and
fondant (royal icing) to add
decorations to your POPs.

Making the cake

This recipe is for a simple chocolate sponge cake that forms the base for the POPs.

YOU WILL NEED 1 stick (125 g) butter, at room temperature • scant ³/4 cup (125 g) superfine (caster) sugar • 2 eggs • heaping 1 cup (125 g) all-purpose (plain) flour • 1 teaspoon baking powder • 1 teaspoon salt • 2 tablespoons cocoa powder • *8-inch (20-cm) cake pan, greased and lined*

1 Preheat the oven to 350°F (180°C) Gas Mark 4.
2 Put the butter and sugar in a food processor, and beat on medium speed until pale and fluffy.
3 Slowly add the eggs as you continue to beat the mixture. Then sift over the flour, baking powder, salt, and cocoa and continue to mix until everything is well combined.
4 Pour the batter into the prepared cake pan and bake in the preheated oven for 25 minutes, or until risen and baked through. Test if it's cooked by inserting a toothpick (cocktail stick); if cooked, the toothpick comes out clean.
5 Leave your cake to cool in the pan for 30–40 minutes, then turn out onto a wire cooling rack for a few hours to cool down completely. Even better, make the cake the day before you want to make your POPs.

CAKE VARIATIONS
Here are some suggestions for different cakes to use as your cake POP base.

Vanilla Cake
Substitute 1 teaspoon of vanilla extract for the cocoa powder. Add your choice of food coloring to the cake if you want a colorful surprise inside the POP. Try adding blue for a Baby POP baby shower (see page 98), pink for a dainty Miss POP (see page 82), or green for a Dino POP (see page 79).

Almond Cake
Instead of a heaping cup of all-purpose (plain) flour, use ¹/2 cup (50 g) ground almonds and ³/4 cup (75 g) all-purpose flour, and add 1 teaspoon of almond extract.

Pistachio Cake
Substitute ¹/2 cup (50 g) ground pistachios and ³/4 cup (75 g) all-purpose flour for a heaping cup of all-purpose flour along with 1 teaspoon of pistachio flavoring. Once the cake mix is made and mixed with your cream cheese frosting, mix in a teaspoon of green food coloring.

Making the cake balls

It's important to make sure that all of the cake balls in a batch are the same size, so use your digital weighing scales for this part. I usually make them 1 oz (30 g) each.

YOU WILL NEED 1 cooled cake (see page 20) • scant ¼ cup (50 g) full-fat cream cheese • 1 cup (115 g) confectioners' (icing) sugar, sifted
Makes 15–20 POPs

1 Put the cake in a food processor and process to form a mixture with a crumb-like consistency. Set aside. Combine the cream cheese and confectioners' (icing) sugar in a food processor until well mixed.
2 Combine the cake crumbs and cream cheese frosting with your hands, until all the frosting is incorporated and you are left with a moist mixture.
3 Measure out 1 oz (30 g) of cake mixture on digital scales. Roll this into a ball and place on a plate. Measure and roll the rest of the cake balls.
4 Put the plate of cake balls in the freezer (with no lid) for 10 minutes until hard, but not rock hard or frozen through. Alternatively, cover the cake balls and put them in the refrigerator for 3–4 hours.

POP TIPS Store your cake balls in an airtight container until you are ready to start molding your POP shapes.
POP TWISTS You can add all sorts of tasty delights to your cake balls to make the POPs even more delicious. Try adding tiny chocolate chips, crushed Crunchy bars, ground nuts, and confetti sprinkles.

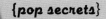

Classic POPs

This is how you transform your cake ball into a plain POP-ready for decorating and becoming a thing of wonder!

YOU WILL NEED 15–20 x 1-oz (30-g) cake balls (see page 22) • 14 oz (400 g) candy melts • • 1 tablespoon vegetable oil • sprinkles, for decoration • *15–20 lollipop sticks*

1 *Put the candy melts into a microwavable bowl.* Microwave on medium heat for about 2 minutes, stirring at 30-second intervals to ensure that the candy melts do not burn.

2 *Once the candy melts are completely melted*, dip the tip (about ¼ inch/0.5 cm) of a lollipop stick into the candy melts, and then insert the stick into the hardened cake ball.

3 *Keep stirring the melts* throughout to ensure that they maintain a smooth consistency. If you find they are too thick, thin the mixture with a tablespoon of vegetable oil.

4 *Holding the end of the stick*, dip the cake POP into the bowl of candy melts, covering the cake POP entirely and using a spoon to help if necessary. Gently shake the cake POP to remove any excess candy melts.

5 *If using sprinkles or sugar-based decorations*, decorate your POP while the coating is still wet. Insert the end of the stick in a polystyrene block or colander while the POP dries. Cover with cellophane and store in the refrigerator.

POP TIP The POPs will keep for a week in the refrigerator or two days at room temperature.

POP art

Once you have mastered making your cake balls and covering them in candy melts, it's time for the real fun to begin— decorating. This is where your creativity can really run wild.

PAINTING POPS

My painting technique has changed since the first book. I no longer use cocoa butters, but instead, have come up with new method—this is the optimum way to create POP designs. Make sure the candy melts on your POPs are completely dry before painting.

YOU WILL NEED
edible dusting powder • confectioner's glaze • dipping solution/rejuvenator spirit • paintbrush • palette or plastic wrap (clingfilm)

1 *Pour some edible dusting powder* onto a palette—about ¼ of a pot for 20 POPs. If you can't find a palette, I find a sheet of plastic wrap (clingfilm) on a plastic board works well. Always be careful with edible paints, because they do stain.
2 *Next, mix together equal amounts* of confectioner's glaze and dipping solution/ rejuvenator spirit, either in an old egg cup (remember, it will stain), or a small plastic bottle, which means you can then keep the mixture for next time.
3 *Carefully add the confectioner's glaze* and

dipping solution/rejuvenator spirit mixture to the powder to form a paste—but don't use all the powder at once. That way, if you have some left, you can put the dry powder back in the pot for future use. Stir with a small paintbrush and then you're ready to decorate your POPs.
4 *Wash your paintbrush with a little washing-up liquid* and handwash immediately. Wash again with washing-up liquid, rinse, and let dry.
5 *To store your colors,* cover tightly with plastic wrap (clingfilm), ensuring that no air touches the paste.

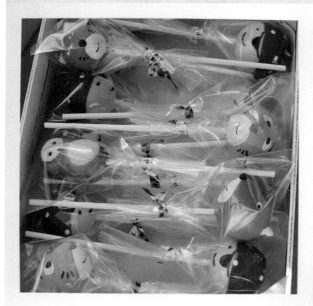

COVERING YOUR POPS
The best way to store your POPs is to cover them with a lollipop cover and place in the refrigerator. These are readily available online (see Suppliers, page 125). I secure my covers with a twist tie. You can add ribbons and labels to the tie, too. Don't leave finished POPs in the refrigerator uncovered as they will sweat.

Sugar Decorations

A simple, yet effective way to embellish your POPs is to add sugar decorations. You can make the decorations by hand or use a mold.

YOU WILL NEED
• fondant (royal icing)
• gum tragacanth
• sugar mold
• edible dusting powders
• paintbrush

1 *Add 1–2 teaspoons* of gum tragacanth to a handful of fondant.
2 *Mix the gum* and fondant with your hands until the fondant feels firm and a little less sticky.
3 *Press the fondant* into a mold and remove immediately.
4 *Dust the shapes* with edible dusting powders (if using). It is best to dust the shapes within half an hour of making them, before they become too dry.
5 *Attach your decorations* to the cake POP while the melts on the POP are still wet; leave the POP to dry.

POP TIP If the fondant gets stuck in the mold, add more gum tragacanth to the fondant.

chapter 1
CUTE & CRAZY POPS

Popsicle POPs

Why have ice popsicles when you can have delicious popsicle POPs? Try the tricolor one first, then experiment with the variations.

YOU WILL NEED 15–20 x 1-oz (30-g) cake balls (see page 22) • 1 package each candy melts in red, yellow, and blue • sprinkles • *15–20 lollipop sticks*

1 Take your cake ball and shape it into a popsicle shape by flattening the ball and molding a flat edge at one end and a curved top. Let harden in the freezer for 10 minutes.

2 Prepare the candy melts (see page 25). Dip the tip of a lollipop stick into the red candy melts and insert it into the popsicle. Dip the entire POP into the melts and let dry.

3 Once completely dry, prepare the yellow candy melts. Dip two thirds of the popsicle into the candy melts and let dry.

4 Finally, dip the top third of the popsicle into the blue candy melts. Let dry for a few seconds and scatter over the sprinkles. Let dry, then cover and store in the refrigerator.

Variations:
To make the chocolate-coated popsicle, shape the cake ball into a popsicle shape, cut out a "bite" from the cake ball, and dip it into dark brown candy melts. Paint the "bite" with white edible dusting powder mixed with confectioner's glaze and dipping solution/rejuvenator spirit. Let dry, then cover and store in the refrigerator.

To make the twister popsicle, shape your cake ball into a cylinder, dip it into white candy melts, let dry, then paint on the pattern using red and blue edible dusting powder mixed with confectioner's glaze and dipping solution/rejuvenator spirit. Let dry, then cover and store in the refrigerator.

Science POPs

Here I show you how to make test tubes, beakers, and conical flasks—a fun idea for a geek-chic party!

YOU WILL NEED 15–20 x 1-oz (30-g) cake balls (see page 22) • 1 package (14 oz/400 g) white candy melts • 7 oz (200 g) candy melts in assorted bright colors • edible black dusting powder • confectioner's glaze • dipping solution/rejuvenator spirit • *15–20 lollipop sticks • palette • paintbrush*

1 *Shape a cake ball into a test tube shape* by rolling it into a thick cylinder and then flattening the top. You could also mold it into a flask shape with a wide bottom and narrow neck. Let harden in the freezer for 10 minutes.

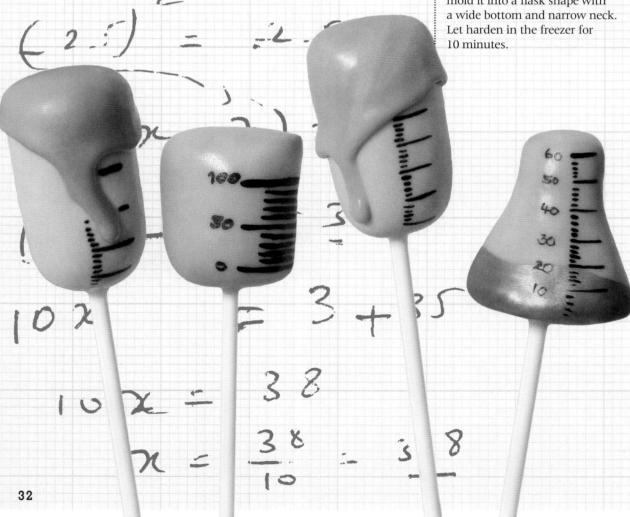

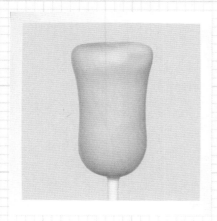
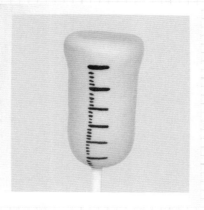
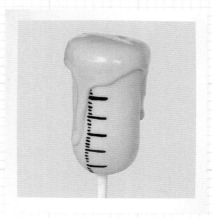

2 Prepare the candy melts (see page 25). Dip the tip of a lollipop stick into the candy melts and insert it into the test tube. Dip the whole shape in white candy melts. Let set.

3 Mix the black edible dusting powder with a little confectioner's glaze and dipping solution/rejuvenator spirit to create a paste, then use it to paint the measurement lines on the front of each test tube.

4 Prepare other colored candy melts—ideally bright and chemical-looking—in separate bowls. Dip the head of one of the test tubes into one of the colors. Shake the test tube a little so that part of the color drips down the test tube. Let dry, then cover and store in the refrigerator.

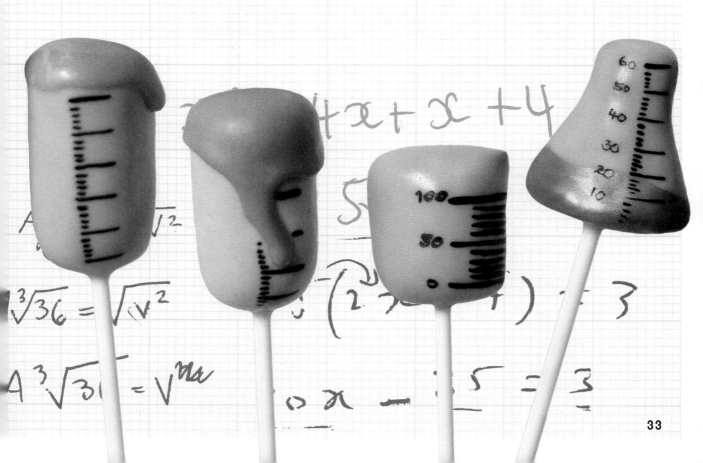

Cake Slice POPs

Aren't these cute? My favorite is the lemon meringue pie—just as good as the real thing!

YOU WILL NEED 15–20 x 1-oz (30-g) cake balls (see page 22) • 1 package (14 oz/400 g) each brown, yellow, and white candy melts • edible dusting powders in brown and yellow, or caramel • *15–20 lollipop sticks • palette • paintbrush*

1 *First, shape your cake ball* into a pie slice. Using a lollipop stick, mark grooves around the outside edge for the pie crust. Let harden in the freezer for 10 minutes.

2 *Prepare the pastry-colored candy melts* (see pages 25). To make the pastry-colored candy melts, mix brown and yellow candy melts together and prepare as normal. Dip the tip of a lollipop stick into the pastry-colored melts, and insert it into the bottom of the pie. Let set.

3 *When dry, dip the top two thirds* of the pie into the yellow candy melts. Let set.

4 *Prepare the white candy melts,* but don't add any oil, so that they have a thick consistency. Dip the very top

of the pie into the thick white candy melts to form the peaks of the meringue.

5 *Using a paintbrush,* brush the caramel-colored edible dusting powder onto the tips of the pie to look like caramelized meringue. Let dry, then cover and store in the refrigerator.

Variations:

To make the cherry cake, first make tiny cherries from fondant (royal icing) mixed with gum tragacanth. Dip the entire cake slice into brown candy melts, let dry, then dip the top and outside edge in pink candy melts. Let dry, then add small dollops of thick white candy melts (see step 4) to create the puffs of cream, and attach the cherries while the melts are still wet.

To make the strawberry cake, make a strawberry from fondant (royal icing) mixed with gum tragacanth. Dip the entire cake slice in sponge-colored candy melts (see pastry-colored melts, above). Once dry, dip the top of the cake into the white candy melts, and attach the strawberry while the melts are still wet. Paint on the jam and cream filling using red and white candy melts to create the "oozing out" effect.

35

Circus POPs

Step right up! Make a POP circus display stand with ringmasters, balloons, and monkeys.

Balloon POPs

YOU WILL NEED 15–20 x 1-oz (30-g) cake balls (see page 22) • 1 package (14 oz/400 g) each blue, red, and yellow candy melts • sugar hearts • *15–20 lollipop sticks*

1 *Take your cake balls* and mold into balloon shapes with a big rounded top and a slightly pointed bottom.

2 *Prepare the candy melts* (see page 25). Insert an upside down sugar heart into the bottom of the balloon using some candy melts to secure it in place.

3 *Let the balloons harden* in the freezer for 10 minutes. Dip the tip of a lollipop stick into the candy melts and insert it into the bottom of the balloon, just behind the sugar heart. Dip the entire balloon into the candy melts. Let dry, then cover and store in the refrigerator.

37

Display Stand

YOU WILL NEED 10 inch (25 cm), 8 inch (20 cm), and 6 inch (15 cm) round Styrofoam (polystyrene) cake dummies • a 12-inch (30-cm) wooden dowel • craft spray paint in blue • adhesive felt sheets in red and blue • paper or card stock • *hammer* • *small saw* • *scissors* • *hot glue gun*

1 *Stack all the cake dummies* on top of each other, starting with the largest dummy.

2 *Hammer in the cake dowel* until it reaches the bottom tier. Lean the dowel on a solid surface and, using a small saw, cut the tip of the dowel so it can't be seen at the top of the display. Alternatively, use the remaining height of the dowel to create the flagpole instead of using lollipop sticks as in step 5.

3 *Next, using the paint spray,* spray the entire display. Let dry for 30 minutes.

4 *While the paint is drying,* prepare the felt bunting. Measure a strip of red felt to fit around the bottom cake dummy (10 inches/25 cm) and, leaving the top of the strip intact, cut out triangles shapes. Peel off the back of the felt and attach the bunting to the bottom cake dummy. Measure a strip of blue felt to fit around the second cake dummy (8 inches/20 cm) and, leaving the top of the strip intact, cut little semicircles along the strip. Peel off the back of the felt and attach the bunting to

the middle cake dummy. Finally, measure a strip of red felt to fit the top cake dummy (6 inches/ 15 cm) and cut out semicircles, leaving the top of the bunting intact. Peel off the back of the felt and attach the bunting to the top cake dummy.

5 *Make the flagpole* by sticking two lollipop sticks together with a hot glue gun or by using the dowel, as mentioned in step 2. Attach a paper or card stock flag at the top of the flagpole.

Ringmaster POPs

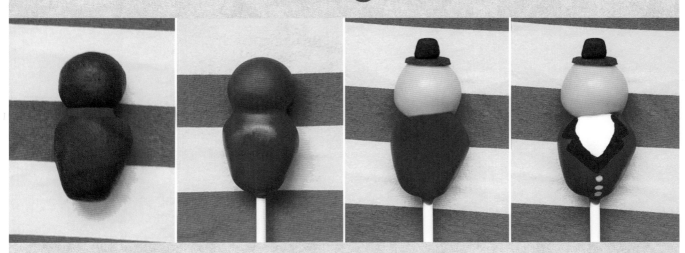

YOU WILL NEED 15–20 x 1-oz (30-g) cake balls (see page 22) • 1 package (14 oz/400 g) each red and pink candy melts • 7 oz (200 g) each black, white, and orange candy melts • black fondant (royal icing) • gum tragacanth • edible dusting powders in white, gold, red, and black • confectioner's glaze dipping solution/rejuvenator spirit • *rolling pin • ½-inch (1-cm) diameter circular cutter • 15–20 lollipop sticks • palette • paintbrushes*

1 *Take your cake balls* and split each one into two balls, one weighing ⅓ oz (10 g) for the head and one weighing ⅔ oz (20 g) for the body. Next, prepare the red candy melts (see page 25). Attach a head to each body using the candy melts. Let them harden in the freezer for 10 minutes.

2 *Dip the tip of a lollipop stick* into the red candy melts and insert it into the bottom of the POP. Dip the entire POP into the red candy melts and let dry.

3 *To make the ringmaster's hats,* harden the black fondant (royal icing) with gum tragacanth and roll it out. Use the circular cutter to cut circles for the rim of each hat. Mold cylinder shapes for the body of each hat. Prepare the black candy melts and attach the rim and body of the hat to each other, using the melts. To make the skin-colored melts, mix ¾ of a bag of pink candy melts, 5–10 white candy melts, and 10 orange candy melts. Prepare as normal (see page 25). Dip the heads into the skin-colored candy melts and attach the top hats while still wet.

4 *Mix each of the edible dusting powders* with a little confectioner's glaze and dipping solution/rejuvenator spirit on a palette to form a paste. Take a paintbrush and paint on the white shirts, red jackets, and gold buttons. Finally, paint on the black bow tie, shirt buttons, lapels, and facial features. Let dry, then cover and store in the refrigerator.

39

Monkey POPs

YOU WILL NEED 15–20 x 1-oz (30-g) cake balls (see page 22) • 1 package (14 oz/400 g) each brown, yellow, and pink candy melts • fondant (royal icing) in red • gum tragacanth • edible dusting powders in white and black • confectioner's glaze • dipping solution/rejuvenator spirit • *15–20 lollipop sticks* • *⅝-inch (1.5-cm) diameter plain cookie (pastry) cutter* • *rolling pin* • *palette* • *paintbrush*

1 *Prepare the monkeys' ears,* at least a day in advance, because they need time to harden enough to be pushed into the cake ball. Harden the fondant (royal icing) with gum tragacanth. Roll out the fondant using a rolling pin and cut out the ears using a ⅝-inch (1.5-cm) diameter cookie cutter. Cut 2 ears for each POP. Prepare the candy melts (see page 25). Dip one side of an ear into the candy melts and attach to the side of a monkey's head. Repeat for the other side. Do this for each monkey and let harden in the freezer for 10 minutes.

2 *To make the monkeys' hats,* harden the red fondant (royal icing) with gum tragacanth and roll it out. Mold cylinder shapes for the hats. Prepare the camel candy melts (see page 25). To make camel-colored melts, mix 1 package of yellow candy melts with about 10 brown candy melts. Dip the tip of a lollipop stick into the candy melts and insert it into the bottom of a monkey's head. Dip the entire POP into the melts. While still wet, attach the hats. Let dry.

3 *To make a fleshier tone for the melts,* add about 15 pink candy melts to the camel-colored melts. Dip the bottom half of the face into the melts for the monkey's mouth.

4 *Using a small paintbrush,* mix each of the edible dusting powders with a little confectioner's glaze and dipping solution/rejuvenator spirit on a palette to form a paste. Take the paintbrush and paint the facial features and the tassel on the hat. Let dry, then cover and store in the refrigerator.

CIRQUE DU PO

Cake Bunting

This baby cake bunting looks adorable on top of a simply iced cake.

YOU WILL NEED bunting template on page 20 • tracing paper • pencil • assorted vintage papers • scissors • glue stick • ribbon, the width of the cake you're decorating • bamboo (wooden kabob) skewers • hot glue gun

1 Trace the template for the bunting and draw the shape onto the vintage paper. For this cake bunting I used six shapes. Cut out the diamond shapes.

2 Lay the ribbon on a table and fold each diamond shape in half over the ribbon. Secure with the glue stick.

3 Tie either end of the ribbon to the bamboo (wooden kabob) skewers and secure with the hot glue gun. Finally, insert the skewers into the cake.

POP TIP
THIS CAKE IS THE SAME AS THE PINK RUFFLE CAKE (SEE PAGE 101) BUT WITH A PRETTY LILAC COLORED FROSTING AND WITHOUT THE RUFFLES.

Sailor POPs

A twist on the classic Russian doll, a nice one for any nautical-themed party.

YOU WILL NEED 15–20 x 1-oz (30-g) cake balls (see page 22) • red fondant (royal icing) • gum tragacanth • 1 package (14 oz/400 g) white candy melts • edible dusting powders in black, blue, and red confectioner's glaze • dipping solution/rejuvenator spirit • *15–20 lollipop sticks* • *palette* • *paintbrush*

1 *First, make the sailor hats.* Harden the red fondant with gum tragacanth and shape a tiny half-moon hat for each POP. Take the cake balls and split each one into two balls, one smaller than the other for the head of the sailor. Prepare the candy melts (see page 25). Dip the head into the candy melts and attach it securely to the body. Let harden in the freezer for 10 minutes.

2 *Dip the tip of a lollipop stick* into the candy melts and insert it into the bottom of the sailor's body. Then dip the entire sailor POP into the melts. While still wet, attach the hat to the top of the head. Let set.

3 *To decorate your sailor,* mix each of the edible dusting powders with a little confectioner's glaze and dipping solution/rejuvenator spirit on a palette to form a paste. Take the paintbrush and paint the facial features and an anchor shape or stripes on its belly. Let dry, then cover and store in the refrigerator.

Hot Dog POPs

Why not make these quirky hot dog POPs as delicious snacks for a summer barbecue?

YOU WILL NEED 15–20 x 1-oz (30-g) cake balls (see page 22) • white fondant (royal icing) • gum tragacanth • brown and pink food coloring • 1 package (14 oz/400 g) yellow candy melts • 7 oz (200 g) brown candy melts • *knife • 15–20 lollipop sticks • piping bag and fine nozzle*

1 *Start by making the hot dog sausages.* Knead small amounts of brown and pink food coloring into the fondant to make a sausage color, then add a little gum tragacanth to harden the fondant. Take a small amount of fondant and roll it into a sausage shape. Use a knife to make a star shape on each end of the sausage. Make a sausage for each POP.

2 *Take a cake ball* and roll it into an oval shape. Press a lollipop stick into the cake ball to make the bun shape. Let harden in the freezer for 10 minutes.

3 *To prepare the bread-colored candy melts,* mix together yellow candy melts with a few brown candy melts, and prepare as normal (see page 25). Dip the tip of a lollipop stick into the candy melts and insert it into the bun. Dip the entire bun into the candy melts, then attach the sausage while still wet. Let set.

4 *Fill a piping bag with a fine nozzle* with the remaining yellow candy melts. Carefully pipe the yellow candy melts onto each hot dog POP to create the mustard. Let dry, then cover and store in the refrigerator.

47

Pencil POPs

An oversized pencil sharpener that I saw in a shop inspired these POPs. Great for an arty party or a student send-off.

YOU WILL NEED 15–20 x 1-oz (30-g) cake balls (see page 22) • 1 package (14 oz/400 g) each candy melts in brown, pink, and white for the wooden color, and as many different colors as you like for the pencils • *15–20 lollipop sticks*

1 Shape your cake ball into a pencil shape: roll the cake ball into a sausage shape and form a pointed tip for the pencil leads. Let harden in the freezer for 10 minutes.

2 Prepare the candy melts (see pages 25) in whatever color you choose (I've used green here). Dip the tip of a lollipop stick into the candy melts and insert it into the pencil-shaped cake ball. Dip the entire pencil into the candy melts and let set.

3 Prepare the wooden-colored candy melts. To make a brown wooden color, mix together white, pink, and a few brown candy melts. Dip the tip of the pencil in the wooden-colored candy melts and drag down tiny zigzags to form the sharpened edge. Once completely dry, dip the very tip of the pencil into the candy melts you used in step 2 to form the colored lead in the pencil. Let dry, then cover and store in the refrigerator.

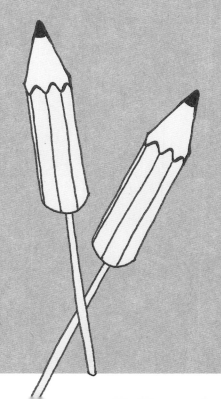

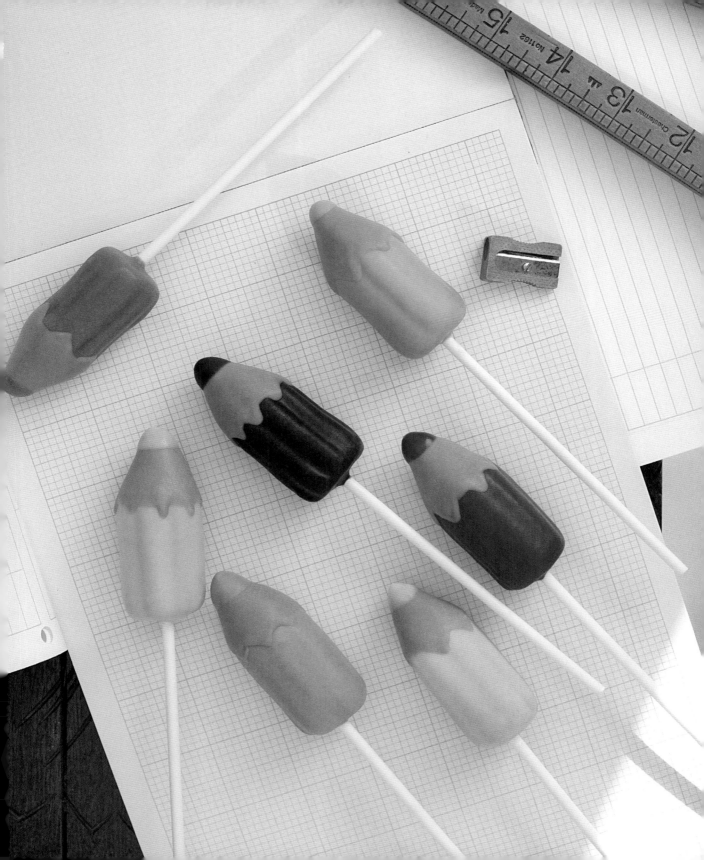

Pinwheels

Instead of adorning a birthday cake with candles,
why not make these decorative pinwheels?

YOU WILL NEED template on page 120 • tracing paper • pencil • pretty vintage paper • scissors • bamboo (wooden kabob) skewers • hot glue gun • button (optional)

1 *Trace the template* for the pinwheels and draw the shape onto the pretty vintage paper. Cut out.

2 *Cut the diagonal lines* marked on the template with a pair of scissors. Fold in the corners to the center of the pinwheel and secure with hot glue.

3 *Attach the pinwheel* to the bamboo (wooden kabob) skewer using the hot glue gun.

4 *Add a decorative button* to the front of the pinwheel, if you want.

Tip:
These pretty pinwheels can be put on top of any cake—this one is the ruffle cake on page 101, but without the ruffles.

Mermaid POPs

These enchanting mermaids are a favorite of mine. Display your POPs in a seashell or treasure chest.

 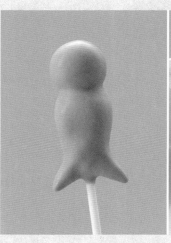  

YOU WILL NEED 15–20 x 1-oz (30-g) cake balls (see page 22) • 1 package (14 oz/400 g) each pink and white candy melts • 7 oz (200 g) each brown, orange, and yellow candy melts • edible glitter • edible dusting powders in green, blue, gold, red, and black • confectioner's glaze • dipping solution/rejuvenator spirit • *15–20 lollipop sticks • palette • paintbrush*

1 Separate one cake ball into two pieces, one smaller than the other for the head. Shape the larger piece into a fish shape for the mermaid's body and tail. Prepare the candy melts (see page 25). To make a pink skin tone, mix together pink and white candy melts and just a couple of brown candy melts. Dip the base of the head into the candy melts and attach it securely to the body. Let harden in the freezer for 10 minutes.
2 Dip the tip of a lollipop stick into the candy melts and insert it into the POP, between the two points of the tail fin, all the

way through the tail and halfway through the body. Dip the entire mermaid into the candy melts until well coated. Let dry.
3 Prepare the candy melts for the hair. Dip the back and top of each mermaid into the candy melts to create long flowing hair. Let dry.
4 Mix each of your edible dusting powders with a little confectioner's glaze and dipping solution/rejuvenator spirit on a palette to form a paste. Using a paintbrush, paint green and blue dusting powders onto the tail of the mermaid and

highlight with a little gold sparkle dusting powder and edible glitter. Paint a red bikini top above the tail. Carefully paint the gold detail on the bikini top, black eyes and eyelashes, and red lips. Be as creative as you like with the remaining mermaids. Let dry, then cover and store in the refrigerator.

53

Paper Flowers

Paper flowers are one of the simplest ways to transform an ordinary room into a party paradise.

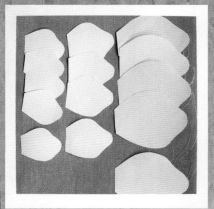 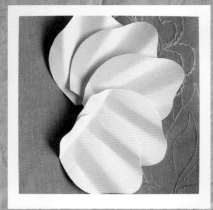 

YOU WILL NEED flower template on page 121 • tracing paper • pencil • card stock or paper in pretty colors (I used white, neon pink, and navy) • *scissors • glue stick*

1 Trace the templates for the petals and draw the shape onto the card stock or paper. For one flower, cut five large petals, five medium-sized petals, and five small petals.

2 Overlap the bases of the five largest petals and stick together using the glue stick.

3 Next, lay the medium-sized petals over the large petals and stick together. Repeat with the smaller petals.

4 Trace the template for the center of the flower and draw the shape onto the cardstock or paper. Cut out the circle and fringe using scissors.

4 Stick the center of the flower in place using the glue stick. Attach the flowers to a wall.

Racing Car POPs

These nippy racing cars are just perfect for a boy's birthday party.

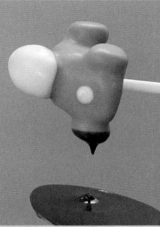

YOU WILL NEED 15–20 x 1-oz (30-g) cake balls (see page 22) • 1 package (14 oz/400 g) each white and black candy melts and other colors of your choice • *15–20 lollipop sticks* • *paintbrush*

1 Split each cake ball into six pieces; shape four small round balls for the wheels, a slightly larger ball for the helmet, and a large semicircle shape for the car's body. Prepare the candy melts (see page 25). Dip each of the wheels in the candy melts and attach securely to the body of the car. Dip the base of the helmet in the candy melts and attach to the top of the car. Let harden in the freezer for 10 minutes.

2 Dip the tip of a lollipop stick into your chosen color of candy melts and insert it into the bottom of the cake POP. Dip the entire POP into the candy melts and let set.

3 Once dry, dip the helmets into the white candy melts, making sure that the candy melts aren't too hot. Let set. Dip each of the wheels into the black candy melts. Let set.

4 Take the paintbrush and, using the white candy melts, paint a small circle on the front of the car for the number plate and allow to dry. Finally, using the black candy melts, paint the visor on the front of the helmet, and the number on the front of the number plate. Let dry, then cover and store in the refrigerator.

POP TIP
MAKE TINY RACING
FLAGS WITH
LOLLIPOP STICKS
AND SQUARES OF
PAPER TO COMPLETE
THE DISPLAY.

Airplane POPs

Personalize these super-cute airplanes for your jet setting friends. I decorated mine with a British flag, an American flag, and a Swiss flag for my Swiss mom.

  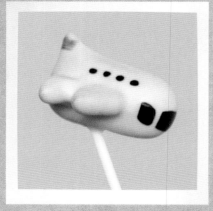

YOU WILL NEED 15–20 x 1-oz (30-g) cake balls (see page 22) • 1 package (14 oz/400 g) white candy melts • edible dusting powders in black and the colors of your chosen flag • confectioner's glaze • dipping solution/rejuvenator spirit • *15–20 lollipop sticks • palette • paintbrush*

1 Make up the parts of the airplane from one cake ball: two large flattened triangles for the front wings, two smaller flattened triangles for the back wings, and a sausage shape with one fat end for the front of the airplane and a pointed end for the tail of the airplane. Prepare the candy melts (see page 25). Dip the base of a large wing into the white candy melts and attach it securely to the lower half of the front of the plane. Repeat on the opposite side, and again for the two back

wings. Let harden in the freezer for 10 minutes.
2 Dip the tip of a lollipop stick into the candy melts and insert it into the bottom of the airplane on an angle (so that it looks as if the plane is taking off or landing). Dip the entire airplane into the white candy melts until well coated. Let set.
3 Using a paintbrush and black edible dusting powder mixed with a little confectioner's glaze and dipping solution/ rejuvenator spirit, paint three windows at the front of the

plane and five smaller windows along the sides above the wings. Paint the flag of your choice on the tail of the plane. Let dry, then cover and store in the refrigerator.

Apple POPs

The perfect gift for a much-loved teacher.

YOU WILL NEED 15–20 x 1-oz (30-g) cake balls • 1 package (14 oz/400 g) green candy melts • fondant (royal icing) in brown and green • gum tragacanth • edible dusting powders in poppy red and gold • *small knife* • *15–20 lollipop sticks* • *paintbrush* • *blusher brush*

1 *Shape the cake ball into an apple shape* and let harden in the freezer for 10 minutes. Mix the green fondant (royal icing) with some gum tragacanth, roll out, and cut out a tiny leaf for each POP. Mix the brown fondant (royal icing) with some gum tragacanth and roll out a little stalk for each POP.
2 *Prepare the candy melts* (see page 25). Dip the tip of a lollipop stick into the candy melts and insert it into the bottom of the apple. Dip the entire POP into the candy melts. While still wet, attach the stalk and leaf to the top of the apple. Let set.
3 *Using a large blusher brush*, dust on the red and gold dusting powders. Cover and store in the refrigerator.

chapter 2
ANIMAL POPS

Cavalier POPs

These adorable mutts will delight any dog-lover.

YOU WILL NEED 15–20 x 1-oz (30-g) cake balls (see page 22) • 1 package (14 oz/400 g) each brown, yellow, and white candy melts • 7 oz (200 g) black candy melts • gum tragacanth • black fondant (royal icing) • *15–20 lollipop sticks • paintbrush*

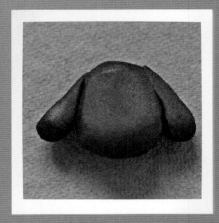

1 First, make the dogs' noses. Mix a little gum tragacanth with some black fondant. Shape pieces of it into small triangles, one for each POP, and let harden. Separate the cake ball into three pieces; one large and two small. Shape the large piece into a head and shape the two smaller pieces into ears.

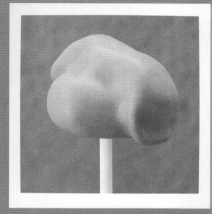  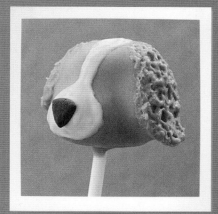

2 Prepare the candy melts
(see page 25). To make a camel color, mix 1 package of yellow candy melts with about 10 brown candy melts, and prepare as normal. Dip each of the ears in the candy melts and attach firmly to the head. Leave to harden in the freezer for 10 minutes. Once hardened, dip the tip of a lollipop stick into the candy melts and insert it into the bottom of the head. Dip the entire POP into the camel-colored candy melts. Let dry.

3 Using thick camel-colored candy melts that have started to set, paint the textured dog's ears. Next, paint the white markings on the face with the white candy melts—making sure that the candy melts aren't too hot.

4 While still wet, attach the black fondant nose to the dog's face. Next, paint on the eyes with the black candy melts. Let dry, then cover and store in the refrigerator.

Turtle POPs

*Just like the turtle and the hare, it's best to take
your time to master making these POPs.*

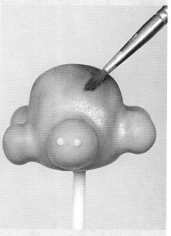

YOU WILL NEED 15–20 x 1-oz (30-g) cake balls (see page 22) • 1 package (14 oz/400 g) green candy melts • 7 oz (200 g) white candy melts • edible dusting powders in black and gold • confectioner's glaze dipping solution/rejuvenator spirit • *15–20 lollipop sticks • palette • paintbrush*

1 *Split each cake ball into six pieces;* one round ball for the body, a smaller ball for the head, and four small balls for the feet.
2 *Prepare the candy melts* (see page 25). Dip one side of each of the feet and the head into the green candy melts and attach firmly to the turtle's body. Let harden in the freezer for 10 minutes.
3 *Next, dip the tip of a lollipop stick* into the green candy melts and insert it into the middle of

the turtle. Dip the entire POP into the green candy melts and let set. Once completely dry, take your paintbrush and dot on the eyes using the white candy melts.
4 *Next, using your paintbrush,* dust the shells with gold or sparkly edible dusting powder.
5 *Mix the black edible dusting powder* with a little confectioner's glaze and dipping solution/rejuvenator spirit on a palette to form a paste. Using

a clean paintbrush, paint the details on the shell, feet, and face, remembering to dot the eyes. (Sometimes, I like to paint eyeglasses on them, too.) Let dry, then cover and store in the refrigerator.

Unicorn POPs

I have always loved unicorns since I was small. Create these magical, mythical creatures for a girly party.

YOU WILL NEED 15–20 x 1-oz (30-g) cake balls (see page 22) • 1 package (14 oz/400 g) white candy melts • white fondant (royal icing) • gum tragacanth • heart sprinkles • edible glitter • edible pearl spray • edible dusting powders in colors of your choice for the mane, blue for the eyes, and black for the eyelashes • confectioner's glaze • dipping solution/rejuvenator spirit • *15–20 lollipop sticks • palette • paintbrush*

1 First, make your magical unicorn horn. Mix the white fondant (royal icing) with a little gum tragacanth and shape it into thin cones, one for each POP.

2 Shape the cake balls into unicorn heads. Start by rolling the cake ball into a sausage shape and bend the head and nose downward. Prepare the candy melts (see page 25). Dip two heart sprinkles into the candy melts and attach to the top of the head, upside down, for the ears. Let harden in the freezer for 10 minutes.

3 Dip the tip of a lollipop stick into the candy melts and insert it into the cake ball, through the neck and halfway through the head. Dip the entire unicorn into the candy melts. While still wet, attach the horn to the unicorn's brow. Let set.

4 Spray the unicorn with edible pearl spray. Once dry, mix the edible dusting powder with a little confectioner's glaze and dipping solution/rejuvenator spirit on a palette to form a paste. Take the paintbrush and paint the blue eyes, black eyelashes, and multicolored mane. Let dry, then cover and store in the refrigerator.

POP TIP
TO ADD GLITTER TO THE
HORNS, DIP THE TIP OF
THE FONDANT HORN INTO
CANDY MELTS THEN
IMMEDIATELY INTO A POT OF
EDIBLE GLITTER POWDER.

Camel POPs

These POPs were inspired by my trip to Jordan. When my sister, Sarah, came up with the idea of using two sticks in a POP, I thought the two-humped camels would be perfect!

YOU WILL NEED 15–20 x 1-oz (30-g) cake balls (see page 22) • 1 package (14 oz/400 g) each brown, yellow, and white candy melts • fondant (royal icing) in the colors of your choice for the blankets gum tragacanth • edible dusting powder in black • confectioner's glaze • dipping solution/rejuvenator spirit • *small rolling pin* • *knife* • *15–20 lollipop sticks* • *paintbrush* • *palette*

1 Start by making the blankets for the camels. Mix a little gum tragacanth with some purple fondant (royal icing) in your chosen color (I used purple and green). Roll out a blanket, 1 1/2 x 2 inches (4 x 5 cm), and mark a fringed edge with a knife. Mix a little black edible dusting powder with confectioner's glaze and dipping solution/rejuvenator spirit, and paint a pattern onto the blanket.

2 Shape the two-humped camel. Form a head with two ears and a body with two humps. Repeat for the remaining camels. Let harden in the freezer for 10 minutes.

3 Prepare the candy melts. To make a camel color, mix 1 package of yellow candy melts and about 10 brown candy melts, and prepare as normal (see page 25). Dip the tip of a lollipop stick into the candy melts and insert it into the bottom of the camel. Repeat with a second lollipop stick and insert it into the camel's tummy. Dip the entire camel into the melts until well-coated. While still slightly wet, attach the blanket to the camel. Let set.

4 Dip the tip of a paintbrush into the white candy melts and dot on the eyes. When set, dot a little of the camel-colored candy melt on top of the white to create the heavy eyelid. Finally, paint on the camel's eyes, nose, and mouth using the black edible dusting powder paste that you made in step 1. Let dry, then cover, and store in the refrigerator.

Fish POPs

Be as creative as you like with these fishy friends—your party display will look great with an ocean of colors!

YOU WILL NEED 15–20 x 1-oz (30-g) cake balls (see page 22) • 1 package (14 oz/400 g) each assorted fish-colored candy melts, such as pink, orange, green, and blue • 7 oz (200 g) white candy melts • edible dusting powders in black, red, and assorted colors • confectioner's glaze • dipping solution/rejuvenator spirit • *knife* • *15–20 lollipop sticks* • *paintbrush* • *palette*

1 Shape your cake ball into a fish shape, making the body a ball with a pointy fish tail. Score through the ball with a knife to make the fish scales. Let harden in the freezer for 10 minutes.

2 Prepare the candy melts
in your choice of color (see page 25). Dip the tip of a lollipop stick into the candy melts and insert it into the fish. Dip the entire fish into the candy melts. Let set.

3 Take your paintbrush and dot on the eyes using the white candy melts.
4 Decorate the fish by brushing some edible dusting powders on it. Mix the black and red edible dusting powders each with a

little confectioner's glaze and dipping solution/rejuvenator spirit on a palette to form a paste. Using a paintbrush, dot the eyes with the black and paint the mouth red. Let dry, then cover, and store in the refrigerator.

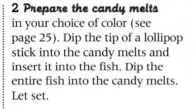

POP TIP
THESE POPS ARE TOO AWKWARD A SHAPE TO PACK UP INTO LOLLIPOP COVERS, SO DON'T TRY THIS AS THEY WILL BREAK.

Dolly POPs

This POP is modeled on my own dog, Dolly. I made sure that the ears were wonky, as this is how she looks in real life.

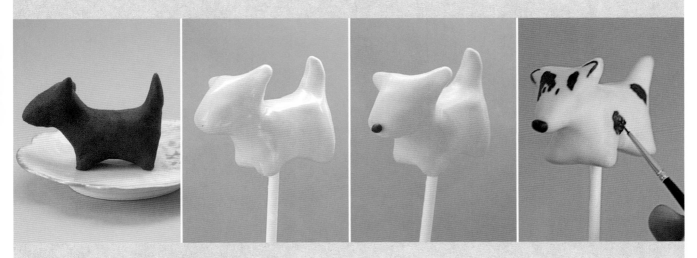

YOU WILL NEED 15–20 x 1-oz (30-g) cake balls (see page 22) • black fondant (royal icing) • gum tragacanth • 1 package (14 oz/400 g) white candy melts • edible dusting powders in black, brown, and red • dipping solution/rejuvenator spirit • *15–20 lollipop sticks • oil • paintbrush • palette*

1 Start by preparing the dog's nose. Mix a little gum tragacanth with some black fondant. Roll pieces into small balls, one for each POP and let harden.

2 Take your cake ball and shape the complicated figure of a Jack Russell. Let harden in the freezer for 10 minutes. Prepare your white candy melts (see page 25). Dip the tip of a lollipop stick into the candy melts and insert it into the dog's tummy. Then dip the entire POP into the melts.

3 While still wet, place the little black nose on the dog's face. Let set.

4 Using a small paintbrush mix each of the edible dusting powders with a little confectioner's glaze and dipping solution/rejuvenator spirit on a palette to form a paste. Take the paintbrush and paint the eyes, patches, and collar. Let dry, then cover and store in the refrigerator.

75

Swan POPs

I think swans are such beautiful creatures.
I'm delighted these turned out to be so pretty.

YOU WILL NEED 15–20 x 1-oz (30-g) cake balls (see page 22) • 1 package (14 oz/400 g) white candy melts • edible pearl spray • edible dusting powders in black, orange, and silver • confectioner's glaze • dipping solution/rejuvenator spirit • *15–20 lollipop sticks • palette • paintbrushes*

1 *Shape the cake ball into a swan shape:* form a long neck with a pointed beak at one end and a tail and wings at the other. Let harden in the freezer for 10 minutes.

2 *Prepare the white candy melts* (see page 25). Dip the tip of a lollipop stick into the candy melts and insert it into the swan. Dip the entire POP into the candy melts. Let set.

3 *Spray with edible pearl spray.* Let dry. Take the paintbrush and brush a little silver powder onto the swan's wings. Next, mix the orange and black edible dusting powders each with a little confectioner's glaze and dipping solution/ rejuvenator spirit on a palette to form a paste. Take the paintbrush and paint the orange beak and black eyes and detail around the beak. Let dry, then cover and store in the refrigerator.

je t'aime i love you je t'aime

Dino POPs

Any little boy would be thrilled to have a herd of Dino POPs to devour at his birthday party!

YOU WILL NEED 15–20 x 1-oz (30-g) cake balls • 1 package (14 oz/400 g) green candy melts heart sprinkles • edible dusting powders in white and black • dipping solution/rejuvenator spirit confectioner's glaze • *15–20 lollipop sticks • palette • paintbrush*

1 Shape a dinosaur from the cake ball: roll the cake ball into a sausage shape and mold a head and body with a long tail. Let harden in the freezer for 10 minutes.

2 Prepare the candy melts (see page 25). Dip the tip of a lollipop stick into the candy melts and insert it into the dino POP. Dip the entire dinosaur into the candy melts. While still wet, insert the heart sprinkles into the dinosaur's back for the spine. Let dry.

3 To decorate the dinosaur, mix each of the edible dusting powders with a little confectioner's glaze and dipping solution/rejuvenator spirit on a palette to form a paste. Take the paintbrush and paint on the white eyes and black nose and pupils. Let dry, then cover and store in the refrigerator.

79

chapter 3
CELEBRATION POPS

Miss POPs

These perfect princess POPs are super-cute with their pretty dresses and pearl tiaras!

YOU WILL NEED 15–20 x 1-oz (30-g) cake balls (see page 22) • 1 package (14 oz/400 g) each pink and yellow candy melts • 7 oz (200 g) candy melts in brown and orange • pearl sprinkles • edible dusting powders in black, pink, green, and red • confectioner's glaze • dipping solution/rejuvenator spirit • *15–20 lollipop sticks • palette • paintbrush*

1 Divide the cake ball into three parts—a small ball for the hair, a bigger ball for the head, and the largest portion, molded into a bell shape, for the body.
2 Prepare the candy melts (see page 25). To create a skin color, mix together pink candy melts with a few brown and orange candy melts until you get the desired skin tone. Dip the base of the head into candy melts and attach it securely to the body, then attach the hair to the head. Let set in the freezer for 10 minutes. Dip the tip of

a lollipop stick into the candy melts and insert it into the cake ball, through the body and halfway through the head. Dip the entire POP into the candy melts. Let set.
3 Dip the hair and back of the head into the candy melts. Add three pearl sprinkles to create the tiara, while still wet. Let dry.
4 Mix each of the edible dusting powders with a little confectioner's glaze and dipping solution/rejuvenator spirit on a palette to form a paste. Using a paintbrush, paint the pink or

green dress, red lips, and black eyes, eyelashes, and dress trim. Let dry, then cover and store in the refrigerator.

Drink Parasols

Add a touch of glamour to homemade lemonade or the tipple of your choice with these chic parasols.

YOU WILL NEED black mini doilies • a sheet of card stock in black• button • pencil • tracing paper • glue stick • scissors • black lollipop sticks • hot glue gun

1 Take a sheet of tracing paper and trace the circle of uncut paper within your mini doily. Trace the circle onto the card and cut out the shape. Mark the center of the circle with a pencil. Using the glue stick, attach the circle of card to the center of the doily and let dry. Cut a slit from the outside of the doily to the center point and bend the doily into a cone shape. Fold the doily into a parasol shape, and using the glue stick, secure the slit shut.

2 Take the hot glue gun and glue the lollipop stick to the center of the parasol.

3 Finally, attach the button to the top of the parasol using the hot glue gun.

Corpse Bride and Groom POPs

Inspired by my trips to Mexico, these are a fun twist on your typical bride and groom POPs!

YOU WILL NEED 15–20 x 1-oz (30-g) cake balls (see page 22) • fondant (royal icing) in assorted colors for the headpiece roses and black for the grooms' top hats • gum tragacanth • 1 package (14 oz/400 g) each white and yellow candy melts • 7 oz (200 g) candy melts in assorted colors (I used red, blue, purple, and orange) • edible glitter • edible dusting powders in black and silver confectioner's glaze • dipping solution/rejuvenator spirit • 1/2-inch (1-cm) diameter circular cutter • 15–20 lollipop sticks • spoon • palette • paintbrush

1 Make the accessories.
To make the roses for the bride's headpiece, harden the colored fondant with a little gum tragacanth, then roll the fondant into little curls—six for each bride POP. To make the groom's top hat, harden the black fondant with a little gum tragacanth and roll it out. Use the circular cutter to cut a circle for the rim of each hat. Mold cylinder shapes for the body of

each hat, then attach the rim to the hat using candy melts.
2 Take the cake balls and split each one into two balls, one smaller than the other for the head. Shape half of the larger balls into bride bodies and the other half into groom bodies. Prepare the white candy melts (see page 25). Attach a head to each body using the white candy melts. Let harden in the freezer for 10 minutes.

3 Dip the tip of a lollipop stick into the white candy melts and insert it into the cake ball, through the body and just into the head. Dip the entire POP into the candy melts. While still wet, add a top hat to each groom. Let set.

87

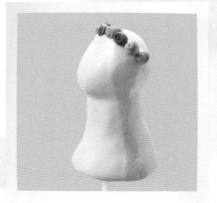

4 Fill a large spoon with the yellow candy melts and dip the back and top of each bride into the spoon for the hair. If you go over the desired area, gently wipe away the excess.

5 Arrange the roses in a wreath shape on the brides' heads while still wet. Let set.

6 Mix the black edible dusting powder with a little confectioner's glaze and dipping solution/rejuvenator spirit to create a paste, then use it to paint on the eyes, nose, teeth, and clothing details. Prepare the red and blue candy melts, then paint on the grooms' mouths and neckerchiefs. Let dry, then using a dry brush, add edible glitter to the neckerchiefs. Add edible glitter to the brides' headpieces in the same way. Using silver dusting powder, brush on the brides' dresses. Let dry, then cover and store in the refrigerator.

Tassel Garland

A particular favorite of mine, these garlands are ultra kitsch and cool—I love them!

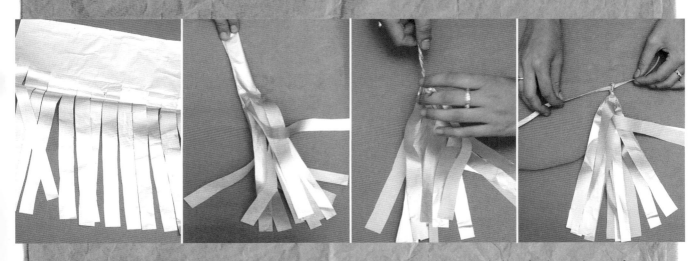

YOU WILL NEED sheets of tissue paper 20 x 20 in. (50 x 50 cm) in your choice of colors • sheets of metallic paper 20 x 20 in. (50 x 50 cm) • scissors • ribbons • hot glue gun

1 First, take a piece of tissue or metallic paper and cut strips vertically up the paper leaving the top 2 inches (5 cm) uncut. Continue cutting all the way along the paper until you have a long tassled piece of paper.

2 Fold the piece of paper in half, in half again, and in half again, until you get a rolled tassled piece.

3 Twist the end of the tassle and curl over so you create a loop. Secure the end of the loop with your hot glue gun. Continue making the tassels until you have enough for your decoration.

4 Take the ribbon and thread your loops on to the ribbon. You can make tassels of all different lengths and with different kinds of materials to create a fun tassel garland.

Piñata

Piñatas look beautiful hanging in clusters. They also act as a mirrorball if you make them with metallic foil paper.

YOU WILL NEED piñata template A on page 122 • pencil • heavy card stock (cardboard) • scissors • tape, such as brown tape or masking tape • wire, such as chicken wire • ribbon or string • foil paper or tissue paper • fringing scissors • glue stick

1 Photocopy piñata template A at 200% to make it the correct size. Use the template to cut six triangles from the heavy card stock. Lay out the pieces as shown and attach them together with tape, as shown.

2 Fold the card stock to make a six-sided box, making sure that you leave a hole at one end.

3 Insert a loop of wire into the hole and secure with strong tape. Thread the ribbon or string through the loop.

4 Cut the foil or tissue paper into strips, each one about 1½ inches (4 cm) wide.

4 Using fringing scissors, fringe the strips of paper, leaving ½ inch (1.5 cm) at the top.

5 Starting at the bottom of the piñata, begin sticking the flat edge of the strips of foil or paper to the piñata, leaving the fringed edges free. Overlap the strips and continue until the entire piñata is covered. Then hang up the piñata, using the ribbon or string threaded through the wire loop.

POP TIP
TO MAKE ASYMMETRIC PIÑATAS LIKE THOSE HANGING HERE, USE THREE TEMPLATE A PIECES AND THREE TEMPLATE B PIECES TO CONSTRUCT THE PIÑATA.

Dress-up POPs

These were inspired by the film "Where the Wild Things Are." I thought Max looked so cute in his costume that I decided to make little kid POPs all dressed up.

Tiger Pop

YOU WILL NEED 15–20 x 1-oz (30-g) cake balls (see page 22) • 1 package (14 oz/400 g) each orange, brown, white, and pink candy melts • edible dusting powders in black and white • confectioner's glaze • dipping solution/rejuvenator spirit • heart sprinkles • *15–20 lollipop sticks • palette • paintbrushes*

1 *Shape a cake ball* into a head shape. Prepare the orange candy melts (see page 25). Dip two heart sprinkles into the candy melts and attach them to the top of the head, upside down, for the tiger's ears. Let harden in the freezer for 10 minutes.

2 *Dip the tip of a lollipop stick* into the orange candy melts and insert into the POP. Dip the entire POP into the orange candy melts and let set.

3 *While the POPs are setting,* prepare the skin-colored candy melts. To make skin-colored candy melts, mix together orange, pink, and a couple of brown and white candy melts and prepare as usual. Pour the candy melts into a spoon and dip the face of your POP into the melts. Let dry.

4 *Mix each of the edible dusting powders* with a little confectioner's glaze and dipping solution/rejuvenator spirit on a palette to form a paste. Take the paintbrush and paint on the stripy tiger details in black. Paint on the eyes in white. Finally, dot the eyes with the black dusting powder paste. Let dry, then cover and store in the refrigerator.

Crocodile Kid

   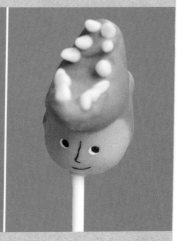

YOU WILL NEED 15–20 x 1-oz (30-g) cake balls (see page 22) • 1 package (14 oz/400 g) each green, white, pink, and orange candy melts • fondant (royal icing) in white • gum tragacanth • edible dusting powders in white and black • confectioner's glaze • dipping solution/rejuvenator spirit • *15–20 lollipop sticks • paintbrushes • palette*

1 Shape the crocodile's head, with a wide open mouth, and leave a round ball at the bottom for the child's face. Let harden in the freezer for 10 minutes.

2 Prepare your candy melts (see page 25). To make a skin color, mix together white, pink, and orange melts (I used half a bag of white melts mixed with 10 pink and five orange). Dip the tip of a lollipop stick into the skin-colored candy melts and insert it into the bottom of the POP. Dip the entire POP into the candy melts. Let dry.

3 Next, make the teeth for the crocodile. Mix a little gum tragacanth with some fondant (royal icing) and shape 10 pointed teeth per POP. Prepare the green candy melts. Dip the top of the crocodile head into the candy melts, leaving the boy's face at the bottom of the head skin-colored. While still wet, attach the teeth to the mouth. Let set.

5 Next, mix each of the edible dusting powders with a little confectioner's glaze and dipping solution/rejuvenator spirit on a palette to form a paste. Paint on the crocodile eyes, nose, and mouth, and the child's face. Let dry, then cover and store in the refrigerator.

Feather Headdress Girl

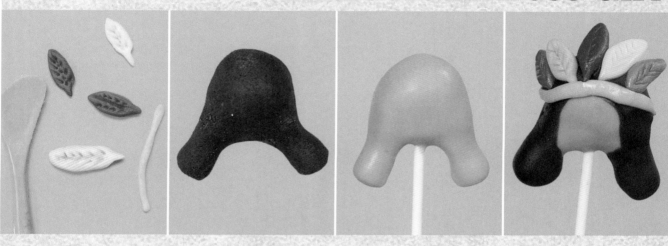

YOU WILL NEED 15–20 x 1-oz (30-g) cake balls (see page 22) • 1 package (14 oz/400 g) each white, pink, orange, and brown candy melts • fondant (royal icing) in a variety of colors • gum tragacanth • edible dusting powders in white, black, and red • confectioner's glaze • dipping solution/rejuvenator spirit • *rolling pin* • *knife* • *15–20 lollipop sticks* • *paintbrushes* • *palette*

1 *Make the headdress.* Mix together a little gum tragacanth and fondant (royal icing), roll out, and cut out individual feathers using a knife. Cut a strip of fondant (royal icing) to be the width of the girl's head.

2 *Take a cake ball and shape* a head with long hair bunching down each side. Let harden in the freezer for 10 minutes.

3 *Prepare the candy melts* (see page 25). To make a skin color, mix together white, pink, and orange melts (I used half a bag of white melts mixed with

10 pink and five orange). Dip the tip of a lollipop stick into the candy melts and insert it into the bottom of the POP. Dip the entire POP into the candy melts and let set.

4 *Next, prepare the brown candy melts* and carefully dip each side of long hair, and the top and back of the head, into the melts. While the hair is still wet, attach the headband and feathers around the forehead, and let set.

5 *Mix each of the edible dusting powders* with a little

confectioner's glaze and dipping solution/rejuvenator spirit on a palette to form a paste. Take your paintbrush and add on the white eyes. Once dry, paint on the black eyes, eyelashes, and nose, and then the red lips. Let dry, then cover and, store in the refrigerator.

Baby POPs

Make these adorable little cherubs for a baby shower or just for fun.

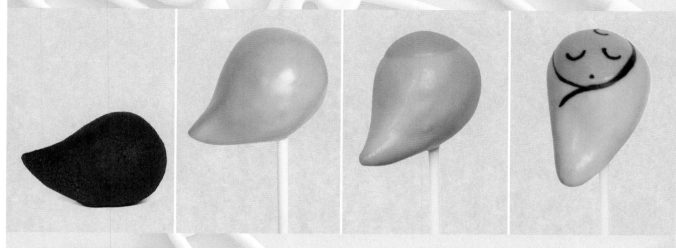

YOU WILL NEED 15–20 x 1-oz (30-g) cake balls (see page 22) • 1 package (14 oz/400g) each pink, blue, yellow, white, and brown candy melts • edible dusting powders in black and pink • confectioner's glaze • dipping solution/rejuvenator spirit • *15–20 lollipop sticks • palette • paintbrush*

1 Shape a cake ball into a baby in a blanket—a rounded cone shape—and let harden in the freezer for 10 minutes.

2 Prepare the pink and blue candy melts (see page 25). Dip the tip of a lollipop stick into one of the candy melts and insert it into the POP. Dip the whole baby in blue or pink candy melts. Let set.

3 Prepare skin-colored candy melts by mixing pink, yellow, white, and a small amount of brown candy melts for a paler skin tone, and use brown candy melts for a darker skin tone. Fill a large spoon with the candy melts and dip the baby's face into the spoon rather than the main bowl. If you go over the desired area, gently wipe away the excess.

4 Mix the black edible dusting powder with a little confectioner's glaze and dipping solution/rejuvenator spirit on a palette to create a paste. Then use it to paint the details on the baby's face: an outline for the face, closed eyes, and a dot for the mouth. Add eyelashes on the girls and a single curl of hair on the boys.

5 Add rosy cheeks by brushing on edible dusting powder in pink with a dry brush. Cover, then store in the refrigerator.

Ruffle Cake

Ooh, this is a pretty cake, and oh so tasty with its swiss meringue frosting.

YOU WILL NEED

For the vanilla cake: 2 sticks (250 g) slightly salted butter • 2¼ cups (250 g) all-purpose (plain) flour • 2 teaspoons baking powder • 1 teaspoon salt • 1¼ cups (250 g) superfine (caster) sugar • 4 eggs • 2 teaspoons vanilla extract • *2 x 8 inch (20 cm) round cake pans*

For the frosting: 1½ cups (175 g) superfine (caster) sugar • 5 large egg whites (1 oz/30 g each) • 4 sticks (450 g) unsalted butter, at room temperature and cubed • 2 teaspoons pure vanilla extract • pink food coloring • a pinch of salt • *heatproof bowl • petal decorating (Wilton tip 104) piping nozzle • piping bags • palette knife*

1 Preheat the oven to 180°C (350°F) Gas 4 and line the two large round cake pans. Put the sugar and butter in a bowl and beat until creamy. Slowly beat in the eggs, one at a time. Continue to mix, and add the vanilla extract. Slowly sift in the flour, baking powder, and salt.

2 Divide the mixture between the two cake pans. Bake in the oven for 50 minutes or until springy and golden. Remove from the oven and leave to cool on a wire cooling rack.

3 To prepare the frosting, place a heatproof bowl on top of a pan of simmering (not boiling) water. The bowl should not touch the water. Whisk the egg whites and sugar in the bowl until the mixture is hot to touch and the sugar has dissolved.

4 Remove from the heat and, using the whisk attachment of a mixer, begin to whip the mixture until it is thick, glossy, and cool. Next, using the paddle attachment of a mixer, add chunks of softened butter to the frosting, mixing continuously until the frosting is a silky smooth texture. If the frosting curdles, continue mixing until it becomes smooth. Add the vanilla extract, food coloring, and salt and mix well.

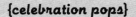

5 Slice each of the cakes in half and spread a thin layer of frosting on the bottom half of each cake. Sandwich the halves together. Next, spread a thin layer of frosting on top of one of the cakes, and sandwich the two cakes together.

6 Using a palette knife, cover the entire cake with about one third of the frosting, leaving the rest for the ruffles.

7 Fill a piping bag with the remaining frosting and pipe figure of eights in columns up the side of the cake. Continue until the sides of the cake are completely covered. Finally, pipe ruffles on the top of the cake.

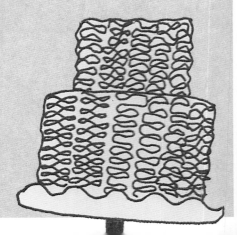

Paper Roses

This is a very simple, yet very effective, PROP to make. I think they look pretty placed in small terracotta pots. You could also display your roses in teacups or little china bowls.

YOU WILL NEED rose template on page 123 • heavy card stock in colors of your choice (I used green, blue, and cream) • *tracing paper* • *pencil* • *scissors* • *terracotta pots*

1 Trace the template for the rose onto the card.

2 Take your scissors and cut out the template.

3 Next, lay the card on a flat surface. Take the outside tail of the card and begin to wind the card in toward the center of the circle.

4 When you reach the center of the circle, cup the rolled card in the palm of your hand, and the card will spring into a beautiful rose. Place your rose in a pot.

POP TIP
AS WELL AS TRACING THE TEMPLATE, YOU CAN ALSO USE THIS AS A GUIDE TO MAKE YOUR TEMPLATES FOR SMALLER AND LARGER PAPER ROSES.

Tiered Cake POPs

Inspired by the wonderful Marie Antoinette film with Kirsten Dunst. I love that scene with all the cakes and all the shoes! Heaven.

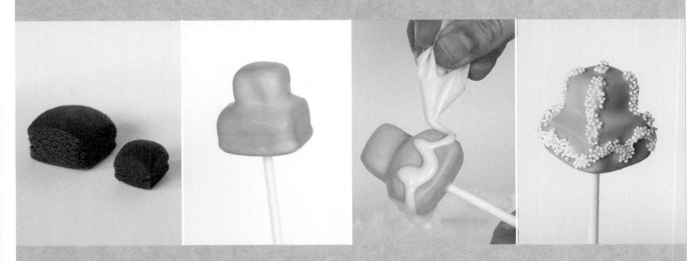

YOU WILL NEED 15–20 x 1-oz (30-g) cake balls (see page 22) • 1 package (14 oz/400 g) blue candy melts • 7 oz (200 g) white candy melts • nonpareils or sprinkles of your choice • 1¼-inch (3-cm) square cookie cutter • ⅝-inch (1.5-cm) square cookie cutter • 15–20 lollipop sticks • small piping bag

1 To make the tiers for the cake, flatten the cake ball and cut out the largest shape using the larger cookie cutter. Gather the remaining pieces of cake ball and push them into the smaller cookie cutter to create the second tier.

2 Prepare the candy melts (see page 25). Dip the base of the top half of the cake into the blue candy melt and attach to the bottom half of the cake. Let harden in the freezer for 10 minutes.

3 Dip the tip of a lollipop stick into the blue candy melts and insert it three-quarters of the way through the cake, so that both tiers are attached. Dip the entire POP into the candy melts. Let set.

4 Fill a small piping bag with the white candy melts. Pipe around the edge of the bottom tier and along the sides. While the candy melt piping is still wet, sprinkle with nonpareils. Let dry, cover, and store in the refrigerator.

POP TIP
EXPERIMENT WITH
SHAPES, COLORS, AND
SPRINKLES TO CREATE
AN ARRAY OF TIERED
CAKE POPS!

Pompoms

Decorate your room with these fabulous paper pompoms and your party will be ready to go!

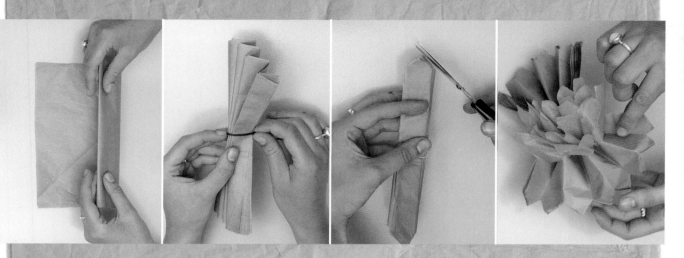

YOU WILL NEED 10 sheets tissue paper, 20 x 30 inch (50 x 75 cm), in colors of your choice • thin floral wire • invisible string • scissors • *makes one pompom*

1 Stack the sheets of tissue paper on top of each other. Make 1½-inch (3.5 cm) accordion folds, and crease the paper with each fold, as if you were making a fan. Continue to fold.

2 Take the thin wire and twist around the center of the folded tissue paper. Trim the ends of the wire. Next, measure the string to fit your display. Tie the string around the center of the tissue paper, on top of the wire.

3 Trim each end of the tissue paper into a point with the scissors. Alternatively, cut a rounded edge for a softer look.

4 Starting with the center, carefully separate the layers of tissue paper until your pompom is complete.

With a selection of POPs,
party PROPS,
and layer cakes, you
can create a stunning
sweet table, just
like this one.

Chocolate Pistachio Ice Cream Cake

Nothing is better than an ice cream cake as the pièce de résistance of any chic party! For a more child-friendly version, simply substitute a cookie for the pistachio macaroons.

YOU WILL NEED For the macaroons: 3 egg whites • a pinch of salt • 3 cups (340 g) ground almonds • ½ cup (50 g) ground pistachios • ½ cup (100 g) superfine (caster) sugar • *baking sheet, greased and lined*
For the ice cream cake: 1 quart (1 liter) chocolate ice cream • 1 quart (1 liter) pistachio ice cream • 40 pistachio macaroons • ½ cup (75 g) ground pistachios • *8 inch (20 cm) cake pan, greased and lined*
For the chocolate sauce: 5¼ oz. (150 g) dark chocolate • ⅔ cup (150 ml) heavy (double) cream • a handful of ground pistachios

1 Preheat the oven to 180°C (350°F) Gas 4 and line the baking sheet.
2 Whisk the egg whites and salt together until stiff. Add half the sugar and continue to whisk.
3 Next, fold in the ground almonds, pistachio nuts, and the remaining sugar until all are combined, taking care not to overmix. Using an ice cream scoop, scoop individual macaroons onto the lined baking sheet. Bake in the oven for 10–12 minutes, until set but not dry. Remove from the oven and let harden for 5–6 hours before making the cake.
4 Spray the cake pan with nonstick spray, or line the base and sides of the pan with parchment paper. Next, break up the macaroons. Line the cake pan with ½ inch (1 cm) of macaroons, reserving some for the second layer of the cake and the final topping.
5 Let the chocolate ice cream soften in a bowl at room temperature for 15 minutes. Next, mix the ice cream with a spatula until smooth, and spread evenly over the macaroon crumbs. Place in the freezer for 45 minutes.
6 Let the pistachio ice cream soften in a bowl for 15 minutes and then mix with a spatula until smooth. Remove the cake from the freezer and sprinkle a second layer of the macaroons on top of the chocolate ice cream. Spread the pistachio ice cream on top of the macaroons and return the cake to the freezer for at least 4 hours.
7 To make the chocolate sauce, first heat the heavy (double) cream in a saucepan, making sure not to boil it. Gradually add the chocolate, broken into pieces, and continue to mix until completely melted.
8 When ready to serve, remove the cake from the freezer, drizzle over the chocolate sauce, and finally, sprinkle ground pistachios on the top. Serve immediately.

Omelie's Chocolate Cake

This delicious treat has always been an absolute staple in our household—a birthday wasn't complete without it!

YOU WILL NEED For the cake: 1 cup and 2 tbsp (150 g) all-purpose (plain) flour • 3 sticks (340 g) butter • 1½ cups (300 g) superfine (caster) sugar • 2 cups (225 g) ground almonds or hazelnuts • 5¼ oz. (150 g) dark chocolate, melted • 6 eggs • 1 teaspoon baking powder • a pinch of salt • *8-inch (20-cm) round cake pan, greased and lined*
For the frosting: 7 oz. (200g) dark chocolate • scant 1 cup (200ml) heavy (double) cream • edible glitter

1 Preheat the oven to 350°F (180°C) Gas 4. Grease and line an 8-inch (20-cm) cake pan.
2 In a large bowl, beat together the butter and sugar until pale. Gradually beat in the egg yolks. Fold in the salt, baking powder, flour, and ground almonds.
3 Break up the chocolate and put into a heatproof bowl over gently simmering water. Let the chocolate partially melt before removing from the heat and

continue stirring until the chocolate is completely melted. Fold the melted chocolate into the cake mixture.
4 In a separate bowl whisk together the egg whites until they are stiff.
5 Fold the whisked egg whites into the cake mixture gently, making sure not to over-fold. Pour the mixture into the cake pan and bake for 50 minutes. Then let cool on a wire cooling rack.

6 For the chocolate drizzle frosting, heat the heavy (double) cream in a saucepan, being careful not to overheat or boil. Break in the dark chocolate and keep stirring until the chocolate has completely melted. Pour the chocolate drizzle frosting on top of the cooled cake. Sprinkle on a little edible gold glitter for some extra magic.

Templates

This section contains all the templates you'll need for the party PROPs. All the templates are printed at 100% so can be traced off the page except for the piñata templates, which are printed at 50% and so will need to be doubled in size using a photocopier.

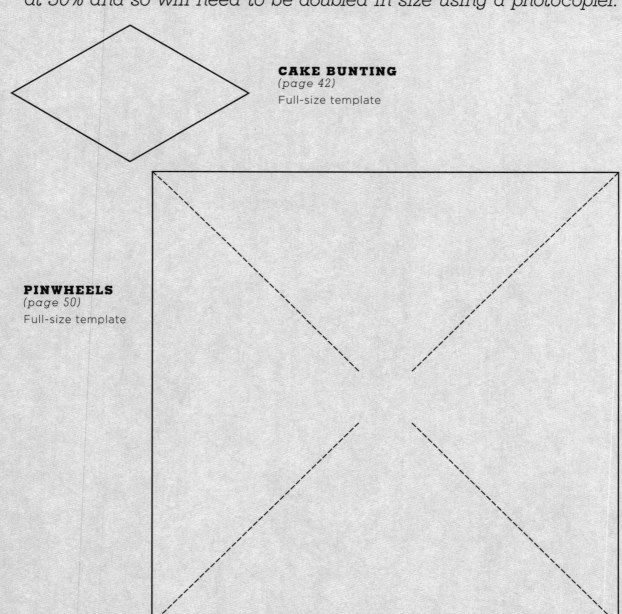

CAKE BUNTING
(page 42)
Full-size template

PINWHEELS
(page 50)
Full-size template

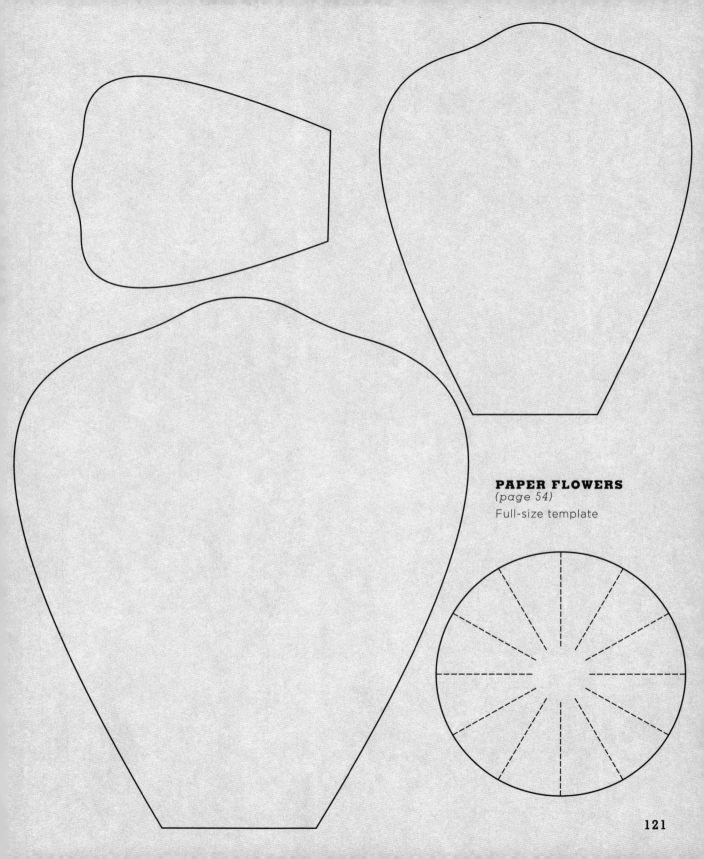

PAPER FLOWERS
(page 54)
Full-size template

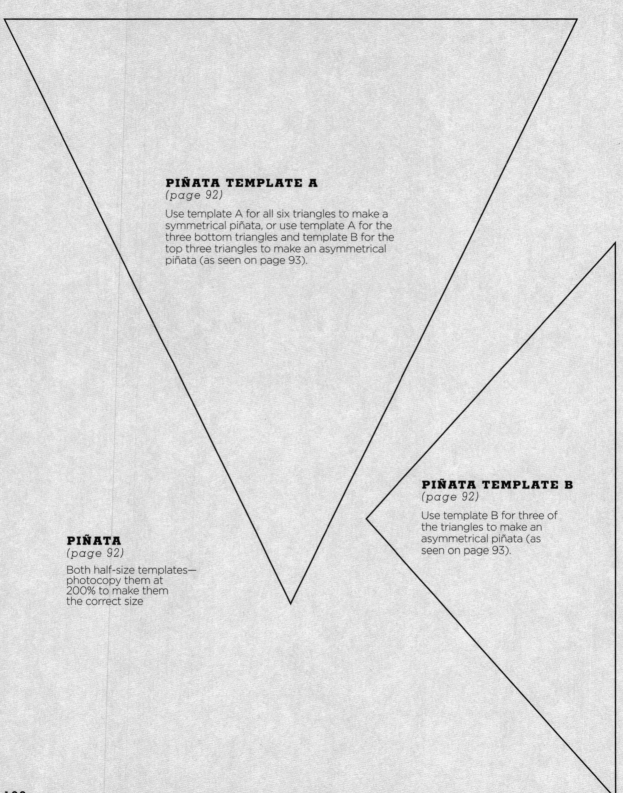

PIÑATA TEMPLATE A
(page 92)

Use template A for all six triangles to make a symmetrical piñata, or use template A for the three bottom triangles and template B for the top three triangles to make an asymmetrical piñata (as seen on page 93).

PIÑATA TEMPLATE B
(page 92)

Use template B for three of the triangles to make an asymmetrical piñata (as seen on page 93).

PIÑATA
(page 92)

Both half-size templates—photocopy them at 200% to make them the correct size

PAPER ROSES
(page 104)
Full-size template

Suppliers

All of the equipment and ingredients used to make cake POPs can be bought from cake decorating suppliers. Be aware that new ingredients appear all the time, so if you spend time browsing in baking supplies stores, you'll pick up new ideas and inspiration.

POP BAKERY
www.popbakery.co.uk
The home of POP Bakery and a great place for inspiration!

US SUPPLIERS

BAKE IT PRETTY
www.bakeitpretty.com
For candy melts, cookie cutters, sugar decoration supplies, and candy molds.

CAKE ART
www.cakeart.com
For lollipop sticks, covers, candy melts, brushes, edible dusting powder, cutters, and sprinkles.

FANCY FLOURS INC
www.fancyflours.com
For display stands, lollipop sticks, and sprinkles.

GLOBAL SUGAR ART
www.globalsugarart.com
For lollipop sticks, candy molds, and candy melts.

KITCHEN KRAFTS
www.kitchenkrafts.com
For sprinkles, lollipop sticks, and candy molds.

MICHAELS
www.michaels.com
For general cake decorating supplies, sprinkles, display stands, and paintbrushes.

NY CAKE
www.nycake.com
For display stands, covers, candy molds, and lollipop sticks.

SUGARCRAFT
www.sugarcraft.com
For display stands and lollipop sticks.

ULTIMATE BAKER
www.cooksdream.com
For sugar decoration supplies and cookie cutters.

WILTON
www.wilton.com
For candy melts, cookie cutters, lollipop sticks and covers, and sprinkles.

UK SUPPLIERS

CAKES, COOKIES & CRAFTS
www.cakescookiesand craftsshop.co.uk
For jumbo sprinkles and gum tragacanth.

THE CRAFT COMPANY
www.craftcompany.co.uk
For candy melts, lollipop sticks and covers, candy melting bowls, and candy molds.

HOBBYCRAFT
www.hobbycraft.co.uk
For candy melts and lollipop sticks.

JOHN LEWIS
www.johnlewis.com
For general cake decorating supplies and candy molds.

KNIGHTSBRIDGE PME
www.cakedecoration. co.uk
For candy melts and lollipop sticks and covers.

LAKELAND
www.lakeland.co.uk
For general cake decorating supplies, sprinkles, and candy molds.

MAKE A WISH CAKE SHOP
www.makeawishcake shop.co.uk
For twist ties, wrappings, lollipop sticks, covers, and sprinkles.

THE PARTY PARTY SHOP
www.ppshop.co.uk
For dipping solution/rejuvenator spirit, lollipop sticks, confectioner's glaze, and candy melts.

SQUIRES KITCHEN
www.squires-shop.com
For gum tragacanth and confectioner's glaze.

SUGARSHACK
www.sugarshack.co.uk
For lollipop sticks, covers, candy melts, brushes, edible dusting powder, cutters, and sprinkles.

Index

Acknowledgments

Nichole was a delight to work with, as always—a dear family friend and brilliant photographer. Valentina, a new addition to the team and an inspirational art director, has embellished the book so much with her wonderful eye. Kamila was a great addition—she made these very cool PROPs for us to display and style the POPs with. Kitty, too, a fellow POPer, helped style two shoots for us, which was fantastic. A special thank you to the rest of the POP team: Suzy, Rebecca, and Tom—all fantastic artists and efficient POPers. **Thank you** to all these talented people for their hard work and expertise. Thanks also to Achillea Flowers (92 Mill Lane, London, NW6 1NL, 020 7431 1727), a beautiful new boutique florist around the corner from POP Bakery, who sweetly allowed us to shoot some of our photos in their lovely store. And, of course, thank you to CICO for taking a risk on us in 2010 (how on trend you guys are!) and being generous enough to offer us a follow up book in 2011. **Finally, biggest thank you is to Ma and Paps**, the best parents ever—poor things had me move out this year for 8 months, and then I came running back to them, couldn't bear being away from POP Bakery and my home-cooked meals—love you too, too much! xxx

Picture Credits

All photography by Nichole Rees and illustrations by Clare O'Connell, copyright © CICO Books 2012, except the following:

Pages 2, 82 (white picture frame) ©iStockphoto.com/Rouzes; pages 5, 32–33 (graph paper) ©iStockphoto.com/wdstock; pages 9–13 (exercise book) ©iStockphoto.com/rusm; pages 11, 12, 13, 115 (vintage photo frame) and pages 101, 112–113 (vintage photography border) ©iStockphoto.com/subjug; pages 21, 42, 45, 46, 57, 69, 74, 89, 93, 104, 109 (speech bubbles) ©iStockphoto.com/Samer Zoran Hindi; page 44 (swimming pool) ©iStockphoto.com/Paul Prescott; pages 55, 91, 111 (pink old paper) ©iStockphoto.com/Agnes Csondor; page 59 (sky) ©iStockphoto.com/Andreea Erim; page 60 (cherry blossom) ©iStockphoto.com/Catherine Lane; page 71 (sheet of papyrus) ©iStockphoto.com/Henning Mertens; page 74 (gold frame) ©iStockphoto.com/Kamil Macniak; page 83 (vector pearl) ©iStockphoto.com/Chris Lawrence; page 117 (fresh leaves) ©iStockphoto.com/ooyoo.